May we never forget

She Is the Moon

To all the women who
have lit the way before us, lifting
our way back to our hearts -
Always remember who you are -
Own all that you are, including your
rage at injustices -
when you walk your talk and speak
your truth you will attract those who
truly resonate with you -
Now go ... grow ... glow!
Love Trish xo

She Is the Moon

A journey of self-discovery

SOPHIE GREGOIRE

2019
GOLDEN DRAGONFLY PRESS

FIRST PRINT EDITION, October 2019
FIRST EBOOK EDITION, October 2019

Sophie Gregoire photo by Studio *Le Carré*

Some of the poems and texts were already published in different forms in 'Rebelle Society' or 'Women's Spiritual Poetry.' In 'Rebelle Society': *Life, Gently; Dear Kindred Soul; The romance of the gardeners; A tale of time; I hope, I create, I become; The heart-break.* In 'Women's Spiritual Poetry': *The Land of Mysteries; Dear Heart; The Things Which Matter; Her Skin.*

ISBN-13: 978–1–7325772–8–2
ISBN-10: 1–7325772–8–5

Library of Congress Control Number: 2019938808

Printed on acid-free paper supplied by a Forest Stewardship Council-certified provider. Cream paper is made from 30% post-consumer waste recycled material.

First published in the United States of America by Golden Dragonfly Press, 2019.

www.goldendragonflypress.com

To the one who brought the Sun.
To all the souls that inspired those words.
To the unwavering support of a mother.
To the medicine woman, the teacher.

To life.
To magic.
In the name of a Journey.

CONTENTS

'I hope that you will go out and let stories, that is life, happen to you, and that you will work with these stories from your life—not someone's else's life—water them with your blood and tears and your laughter till they bloom, till you yourself burst into bloom. That is the work. The only work.'

—CLARISSA PINKOLA ESTES

You are not what happened.

You are the way you took to come back.

You are the magical path—

it is made of secrets, candles, wildflowers and strength

that you walked to recover.

Introduction

This book is a collection of poems, discoveries and thoughts that I wrote on a journey back to myself. Those words were written in many different places of the world and at different times between the years 2015 and 2018. They travelled with me.

They are abrupt, inconsistent and scattered sometimes. As if we could only retrieve who we are and reveal our own puzzle by regathering pieces, both out there in the world—and deep inside ourselves, in the recesses of our psyche.

They are displayed here as they sounded right and organized in the light of today, and not properly in a chronological manner because, this is a story of many spirals and often we come back to old lands to find something new.

‘Do not choose the lesser life.
Do you hear me.
Do you hear me.
Choose the life that is yours.
The life that is seducing your lungs.
That is dripping down your chin.’

—NAYYIRAH WAHEED

Poetry

The Journey to the Heart

This poem was written as a sacred ode of devotion to my own heart. To its true desires, aspirations and calling. It was a promise, almost an offering that one makes at the start of a journey. A promise of remaining true to myself, true to what matters, true to the inner symphony.

Dear Heart,

I still don't know,
How we may feel
On our way to hopes,
On the road to dreams.

Still wondering,
If the sun will always
Set over our songs that alight,
Every breath
Make our pulse,
That lively.
But I do hope,
Sweet Lady Heart
That until the end
Of all dawns,
You'll feel magic.

Dear Heart
Still wondering
Which grounds,
Our paces may tread upon
Which oceans,
Our eyes may caress
By which sunset,
We may be tucked in.

But at least
I do hope
At heart,
You'll see, discover and learn

How close we all are
On every little side
Of our swinging world,
Aerial blends of shadow and light
All, each of us,
Climbing the mountains of dreams.

Still wondering,
Whom we may love.
Whose kisses,
Which sparkling smiles
Whose hands,
Which witty one.
But I do wish,
At heart
Symbiosis
Will be deep
Your slightest atoms,
Awakened.
Spring-blooming,
Till purple blood.
Jumping of joy
You and Him,
Roads to the sky
As dancing wolves
Under bright moon
Painting desires
The eyes lit up
Lit up and filled,
Filled with stars.

*

Sweet lady,
Still wondering
Which souls,
We may come across.
If far from our own melody,
They'll try and drive us.

If windows to the world,
They'll try and shut down.

Perhaps,
Soul-liars and heart-players
On the way, we'll glimpse,
But I do hope
At heart
Sweet lady,
You'll understand, forgive, forget and leave
Walk away from roses thorns,
Instead of judging.

Lovely wanderer,
I hope
Gypsy at heart that you'll stay.
Now and then,
Here and always.
That you will never build borders
Over the seas.
But multicolour,
Sweet, bold ribbons
Thrown all around,
Around our colourful world
And
As our own rhythm,
You and I.

*

With all heart
Dear Heart,
I do wish
Our love never fades.

May I always,
Hold and cherish
These secrets of yours.
Art fantasies or purple nights
Lust for freedom or sunflowers

As you wish,
Dear Lady Heart.

Hoping,
I will be bold enough
So that my eyes,
Can speak your words.
And my hands write
Over the novel of life
In your most favourite
Treasured,
Calligraphy.

Dear Heart,
May we never forget
Both you and I.
As long as
We will be intertwined,
Lovers at all times.
As long as you'll unveil,
Each day
Every hour,
Your enchanting words
To me
I give you my word:
A pink cheerful promise
I'll do my best
Always and forever,
To make them live.

Sweet Lady Heart,
Ache sometimes we will
For sure
But lightly,
Though.

I believe...
Hearts don't really suffer
When in search,
In search for their golden dreams.
Dear Heart

My love of all times,
I hope we choose
You and I,
Now and always
Here and above the seas.
Our own ways over theirs
Love poems over walls
Fire over safety.
And above all
May we hold in our Heart,
Sunsets over diamonds
Life, over fear.

You are always more free than you think,
and freedom is a choice.
Freedom is a leap.
Freedom is the decision to walk the magical road.
It is a joyful and inspired adventure,
it is a golden prayer into the unknown.

The Land of Mysteries

This poem was written as I was deciding to leave France, and many of the foundations, situations and loved ones that were my life before the Awakening.

There is no more, here,
To see.
There is no more, here
To breathe,
Darling.

The City of light is city of ghosts is city of sanctuaries.

One day, possibly,
When on top of the mountain of dreams
We'll be back,
Dear Country.

Country of our first walks,
Infant steps
Gently hopping,
Dear Provence.
Our untameable ocean waves
The wavy hair of the free ones,
Our first bike-rides.

Oh, how much we've smiled there,
How much we've laughed
How much we've loved
Oh how sunny France once was,

The unforgettable countryside tracks.

Oh, how much we believed in living at a standstill,
When we had no wings.
How life could have been simple,
If we had no calling.
How far away
In space and time,

They now all seem.
But forever dancing in my mind
Beauties stopped in time
My frozen statues of smiles.

Of course,
Love
Still.

But need to go
Soon,
You know.

The ways less travelled,
The unnamed roads
The leap of the traveller,
You knew.

Yes, it's a Goodbye,
To the Land of Mysteries.

But maybe some time,
In this life
Or in another shot of time,
I'll be back.

When words spoken
Light handled
Love given
To other needing hearts,

When I have come full circle.

One day
Dear Country,
When I know why on Earth
I've come on Earth that time
With such a mind full of dreams,
I'll fall,
Once again
For the hundredth thousandth time
Under my olive trees' stars,

Smell the set-in-stone perfume
Our first strolls.

My parents' gazes
The radiant ski slopes,
The unforgettable smiles.

And I'll rest,
Quietly
Mattress of lavenders.

Surrounded by a bunch of kids with blue eyes,
And that day
In their bewitched looks,
I'll read
I'll find
I'll catch
Tiny sparkles of light
The letters,
Of
Our
Whys.

'The death of childhood is the beginning of poetry.'

—ANDREI TARKOVSKY

'I'm so glad I live in a world where there are Octobers.'

—L.M. MONTGOMERY

The Melody of Time

This poem was written in honour of my grandmother, who left this Earth too soon. She played a significant role—happy, nurturing, soft and purple, in the France of my youth.

That is true,
we never had the time
to smile enough
go and bite the sun
tell our stories,
and narrate each other.

Of course,
you did leave
even before I bloomed,
before I could make words
out of the petals of my thoughts.

Of course,
You never got to see
that little brunette you created.

Live, grow up,
suffer and love.
Climb her ladders and fall,
jump on trampolines
like an amused gazelle,
stride along dark limbo
flowering our world,
with new ideas.

Of course, I know
we never could,
Remember and relate
in concert
the sweet novel
of our past.
The aniseed sweets

Our cushiony days,
but also the dramas
the hollers and adventures
that adorned our lives.

Time did fail,
forever cutting the thread.

Ethereal and transparent
Saturday,

You flew away.

*

I still remember our August's stars,
yesteryear's perfume
and our raspberry scents,
the candies
and crystals of violets.
I have inhaled your recollection
inside and out,
I have surrounded them.

Sensing you around me
Still
Waiting,
in one room or another.
Timidly,
Discreet
Gently
Loving,
The books of childhood
The music of a teen,
every time I wander back.

On that sad and bitter day,
Reminding us of your leaving hour
The day you departed
for the Infinite sea,
I have come to thank you for your gifts.

Hoping you will hear my words
from where you may stand
Unalterable star,
Shining a bright blue sky.

There are those souls who do not flee,
spirits who do not become ghosts
in any way and whatsoever,
time speaks.

✶

Deep inside,
I know you listen
hear, help, smile
and laugh at my mistakes
Follies, smiles, and wanders.

We now stand apart
Maybe,
like seasons do.
In a way,
energetic summer and stationed winter.

But the more
time offers us its days,
entrusts us with
its round hours,
white unlimited treasure to decorate.
The more I hear,
your sweet voice
blue and purple waves
love
velvety, downy melody,
softly,
relating.

On that sad and bitter day
Reminding us of your leaving hour,
The day you departed
for the Infinite sea.

May a thousand singing birds,
surrounded with baskets
of Lilly of the Valley
flow along your way.

Carrying in their scented petals,
all our summer memories
and sunset skies,

With Eternal love.

I love her, and that is the beginning and end of everything.'

—FRANCIS SCOTT FITZGERALD

The highest form of Sacred Marriage,
would it be physically visible or not,
is when two souls incarnate together
to help each other remember their gifts and truth,
and their ancient promise of being of Service.

Life, Gently

This poem is dedicated to the waves of love. To its rising and its movement. To its birth, falling and reawakening. To a heart's music.

Our lines crossed
Doomed to meet I would say,
I don't believe that much in fate.

What a gaze,
what a smouldering look.
Fireworks set alight
from words to eyes,
from flaws to souls.
Haven't we always known each other?
Darling, kiss me passionately
Oh yes, we have.

Swinging beats and songs
in my head,
so cheerful
they carry me,
he carries me.
In his sparkling eyes,
I see our respective lines
chasing one another,
flirting, weaving around
and finally gathering in a blazing kiss.

No more fears,
only awaken boldness and audacity,
we're kings of the hill.

✶

Stop.

How harsh life can be
pulling us out of our dreams
yet it looked so tangible,

so real.
Slamming doors.

On that winter day, he left.
His words, forever remembered
Stated so strongly,
Unwavering
Even his face, unfazed.

I'm falling down,
down from our cliff's summit.
God, I'm almost dead,
shattered into a thousand pieces
pieces of myself everywhere,
divided all around
strewed and lost
among endless tears.

No, there must be a way,
of course, there is way,
a way to have him back.

Oh, dear me,
I'm afraid you had refused
to hear the signs, his signs,
but you knew, intimately knew,

He was a butterfly.

✶

First came anger,
Hey boy, did you think
you would bring me down
that easily?
Of course, I have my own resources,
don't you know that?
I won't try to spy on you,
to accuse you, to hurt you back.
Don't drive me down that road,
to your road
I'm better than that.

Afterward,
sadness knocked on the door.
Tireless sorrows,
clinging to me
as a second skin,
energy-sucker.
I'm nothing but anxiety,
jammed knot in my stomach.
You are there
when I wake and when I fall asleep.
An evasive shadow,
chasing me like a hunted wild animal,
even stalked in my dreams.
Honey, please go
let me walk alone,
but deep inside

I'm looking for your face
on every street,
was it you?

Holding on to our memories
like a terminally ill person
to a last remedy,
nothing will be tidied
in our flat, nothing moved,
or reorganized.

We never know!

✶

That girl he fell in love with,
I can't find her anymore
where is she,
where has she gone?
Lost.

Have I dreamt?
I'm nothing anymore
no one anymore at all,
only scared

scared to death.
Cold nights,
days and weeks
lonely days,
empty nights.
No recovery.

*

Oh, dear me, my little doll,
what about acceptance?
How many hours have we
spent savouring our sadness,
trotting out our sorrows
repeated thoughts played in a loop.
Was it worth it?

Look, all around you
the world keeps going.
They all go out,
smile, dance, and laugh.

Sun, rain, night.

They make it even harder,
spiking as a needle,
freezing pain.
Unshared
Won't there be an echo?

No, nobody hears
your suffering.

It's spring.
Trees are getting new leaves
Even your favourite iris
are blooming.
No, they haven't grasped it.
Haven't heard your call,
your call for life around to stop
to wait a little more,
for you to be back.

Dear me,
they won't come and rescue you.
You need to get through this alone,
you alone.
Oh no, don't cry,
stop crying
breathe,
gently.

✶

Little doll,
what about closing the chapter?
Anyway, look, it's all scrawled
filled out,
the page of your story with him.
All your evenings, nights,
they all have been repeated
even relived in dreams.
The page is all covered with tears.
No more free space to write,
no more things to say.
We have no choice, you see.
Anyway, we don't have time
no more hours,
minutes are more precious.
Trying to talk to him
to understand
yes, you've tried,
tried enough.
Your efforts,
like messages in a bottle,
lost energies.
Attempts to put a word,
a rationality on things
all failed,
declared as missing.

Come on, little doll,
it's in your hands.

Come and walk with me.
Let's go back to life,
back to life again.
Readjusting.
People, friends,
smiles, laughs, birds.

Life. Gently.

Yes, it was a long adventure,
the return of the
solitary castaway!

Of course, less and less though,
it still hurts, I still miss him.
There is no rush my little doll
take your time,
please take your time.
Breathe.
Breathe again
Smell the flowers,

Courage is the only thing you need.

✶

Time and battles and victories
It's becoming past.
He is becoming past,
nothing more than the previous point of the line.

No, let's not erase your memories
press Delete,
throw them away to the sea.
They are yours too,
You too.
Let's keep the positive,
the enthusiastic moments.

He is not evil,
just a man
entitled to go,
to leave.

No, let's not throw
everything away,
gifts, pictures,
witnesses of your love.
They're just things
emotions, reflections,
and witnesses don't die
when the crime is ending.

Oh, my little doll!
Here you've climbed at last, all alone.
What an amazing view
we now have from the top
of that mountain,
How unexpected.

You're happy again,
existing again, released.
It's so quiet here,
so relaxing,
a bubble bath.
Can you feel now
at last,
the scent of your dear lavender?
Can you feel now,
the enveloping warmth
from your cherished sun?

The line is waiting.
Now ready to be drawn
and filled with another story.

*

Yes, that's true, darling,
our lines met, overlapped.
But they now follow
their own roads,
their own dreams.

Surely they'll twirl around again,
cheerful whirls.

Somewhere else,
with someone else, as butterflies
Aren't we both butterflies?

Let's face it, wasn't it exactly,
That freedom
That I loved in you?
A man with no tie.

I'm ready.
Look, it's as old as the hills...
Let our lines separate,
gently, quietly.
As inexorably as they intertwined.

It's time,
Butterfly of colours.
Good morning.

'No one but a woman in love ever sees
the maximum of men's greatness.'

—ANAÏS NIN

Dear Kindred Soul

Dear Kindred soul
At heart,
I am pretty sure
I will never get the chance
to tell you any of this.

Neither the chemistry
I felt on every part of my skin
the warming shivers,
That shake my pink
and spring waiting heart
when we first met.

Nor how you made me feel
Spreading your twirling light
and wildfire,

Deep down,
body and heart.

Neither the roads you opened
standing on your sweet boldness,
nor the energy you gave
handing over strength
and dreams and leaping potentials,
your laughing world of thoughts
to me.

I am almost certain
you'll probably never know
to what extent, and for how long,
our shimmering recollections
have hoisted on my cheeks,
such a festive smile.

Was it days, months
or maybe years?
I can't even recall,

when it, we started,
you see.

Time is a treacherous joker
Isn't it misrepresenting our reality?

Placing kindred souls
so far away on its merciless calendars
while the mind still recalls,
draws the thread of the past
weaves extensions from it
a while, such a long while after,
time speaks.

Evidently,
the heart still jolts,
the soul still dances
its most rousing summer melodies,
when you come around
for an imaginary wander.

*

In the tangible word,
I know I may see you again,
But deep down
I doubt it.

Even if I bump
into your light-green gaze
I do know,
and that's so dreadful,
I will never see you again.

I could catch a glimpse of you,
as a shape or an outline
walking down a well-known street
But,
I get the feeling
and it is killing
my entire gentle and childish heart,
I will not reach

the former you,
your well-known reflection.

If it is meant to be like this,
I'd rather not see you again.

No, I prefer to remember
our yesteryear soul connections,
Your hands in mine
as ribbons to my heart,
our sacred vestiges of an old past
Beautifully buried recollections.

✶

Those pictures
Live
inside my velvet secret box
Defying time,
its cold and claimed reality.

In that jewellery case of my heart,
you have been put in line
or shall I say on top,
among all the kindred spirits
of all times.

You simply dazzle,
the centre of the whole limelight.
As shiny as our rainbow moments,
brilliant as your words
their waving echo,
a sweet ballet dancing
of my mind.

I prefer keeping you there
not to fade our past,
with a less lovely novelty.

I don't need the new you.
He must be altered by time,
by the mysteries life

put on his road,
Its whispered follies.

Maybe we will meet again,
unannounced.
One day I'll be in a good mood.

Admittedly, that's true
It wouldn't be you, me, us anymore.
Life doesn't preserve
It moves, shapes, destroys
and rebuilds its garden.

But, who knows?
There's a chance our beings
could get on well,
Some kind of us could be reborn
if you bring an
incredible magic wand.

Maybe our former magnet,
would inexorably gather us once more.

Your smouldering looks,
would still remember
how to fondle my body and soul.

You would undress my heart,
Your expert touch.

You would read,
behind my impish and smiley eyes
and this wavy hair you loved that much,
messed by the same sun
the same wind,
These genuine thoughts of mine.

Have you also kept in your secret box,
the keys, the passwords and decoders
that allow to reach
my twirling and vivacious realities?

And I can feel now,
writing these unexpected lines
of eager words,
I would be happy
I think,
if we met again.
To catch your words,
spruce and arabesque music,
feel your rainbow skin,
receive the enveloping smiles
That time, elsewhere,
than in daydreams.

Where are you hiding?
That space between
the strength of the past
and the promise of the future?

I will meet you there.

And he was standing there, like a crazy man.

And the only thing I could think of was—

I love you.

The Heartbreak

You are
The heartache.
But my breath,
Still won't
Let you go.

You are
What's left,
With no answers
The questions
With no name,
Almost exhaled
Without hope
Symphony froze on play,
In between gazes.

You are
The bravery,
Of the wait.

Years and centuries of time,
It seems
Sitting in the middle of a green field
Wildflowers blooming,
Expecting a touch.

You are
The madness
Of me.
A black hole of ages,
Only for
The splendour of a word.
When?

I set alight
At night,
The candle
Of our love.

It dances,
Slowly praying.

Your words,
Never speak your letters
Your hands
Fly so high,
But your mouth
Moves backward when you speak.

I can hear
Our love
Breaking away,
The rhythm of a funeral.
Why?

You are
A painting,
Wildly lying on the wall
You tell a story
Could be unchanged,

But your colours
They vibrate
In your twirling mind,
And the story of your shapes
Always varies.

In the rise and fall,
The expectations never fulfilled
Along the minutes, hours, or days
Of a road with you,
Windy
You seem to stand
On top of shadows and light realms,
Smiling
Are you real?

The planets,
Softly pulling our threads
They do know,
Trust me

Your manners,
Your tricks.
Witchery?

You are
The teacher.
The challenge,
Behind the breakdown.
The reasons,
Behind the tears.
The way
The thread
The line,
Of the path.

The void of my heart,

Love or magic?

Medicine Woman,
Don't be afraid, when the time has come
To claim your angel blood.

Don't veil, once again, don't tame
The healing power of your hands
The mystery touch of your skin.

Don't wait, Lady
For the gifts are heard, you are seen
Wherever you are, already.

Don't turn back, ever
For your sacred blood is the wave that moves us all
Your depth, the sanctuary
Your words, the shield.

‘We travel, some of us forever
to seek other states, other lives,
other souls.’

—ANAÏS NIN

The Fall of the Soldier

The poem written in Jerusalem relates the experience of death and of the dark night of the soul we may experience on a spiritual journey. When we have lost and left so much, deliberately and in the name of truth—but haven't found our new landmarks yet.

Lovely wanderer,
How far you've travelled.

Do you recall
What life was, before the leap?

I know
It didn't feel true, it wasn't you
Heart burning,
I remember.

The doors,
To quit.

How inspiring it seemed!
How many,
Golden and green hopes
Were they hiding?

The bougainvillea trees.

Walk, Soldier
Your heart was whispering,
Set out.
Love, peace, gold even
You were seeking.

The gold of the heart
The peace of the soul.

So you braved
Every danger,
Sweet revolutionary.

Your weapons were flowers,
Dances and streamers!
You braved the world
By way of poetry,

Your pastels.

No,
As long as life couldn't
Play your heart's song.
No,
You had to walk a little further
To open doors,
Win other battles.

Become Lion,
King of the hearts
Thinker of words
Paintbrushes' player.

No, for sure
You thought.
The world must be breathing,
That same sweet air of yours,
Somewhere.
Embrace
That same ardour,
It had to

Gold! You were seeking.

✶

How beautiful it is to believe,
The conquest, the New World
We would be 100, we would be 1000!
There would be painters in the streets
We would water sunflowers,
And
Maybe,
He would be smiling.

The green walks were magnificent,
At that time when you didn't know
What was behind the doors,
After the leaps.

How brave it was, Soldier.
How much your eyes were shining
Even the sun,
Was hiding!

But couldn't you see?

That our world is lies
That people are pretending
Sleeping on that bed
That you're fighting alone,
Opening doors, going off to crusades
But no one desires, to follow
To see.

How sweet, tender and smooth
Was it to dream.

✶

And who knows?
Were you thinking.
Maybe, even
You'll find once again
Your green walks,
That cheerful hope of your heart?

Clock is ticking,
The cycle of seasons
It's already late,
Trenches.

Your insouciance,
Turned into balloon
You're fluttering in the wind.

How beautiful were those skies,
Of yours.
So many sunsets, have you painted

So many hearts have you heated up,
Your weapons, your words,
How beautiful was your Asia!
At that fecund time of the green walks.

✶

That's ok,
Soldier
As long as you're alive,
Warrior of the hearts
Even if you fought for a world,
That couldn't see.

Youth.

But the radiance of your eyes
Can you feel it?
It's flickering.

Your fire is dying
Lay down, your weapons
Your smiles, your paintbrushes
Every dance,
Knows a curtain of its own.

See, that candle
Its pale glimmer, it's sinking.
Lay down your letters, your poems,
Your light
Behind the stones, the churches.

See, Soldier
You're dying.

Leaving, in arabesques
You're bowing out, ballet dancing
You're flitting around

Once again, always because you never could
The angles, the squares.

How beautiful it was to dream!
Your green strolls.

How grand it is,
Almost sacred
To pass away, that way
At the back of a grey church.

Here comes winter.

How brilliant were your songs
So much sun,
Soldier!

Your ardour, but how old were you?

Entertaining wandering thinker.

Lay off your flowers, your orchids
Your smile, your pens
Up in the air
Don't jump! It's winter,
They have flown away.

✶

Here you stand, tonight
At the back of that country church.
Here is your linden.

The formerly smells, your green strolls, you're gone. Your light is flickering, Soldier.

Today,
You're 1,000 years old.

Even the grey country
Yet,
Has wiped out your name.

There is a part of strength that we can only build
in the spaces of aloneness,
where the only support system is ourselves.

The Things Which Matter

When all is said and done,
All the chapters written.
When the sun sets its last dance
Away,
The book closed.

When the endless night comes,
We'll remember
The way we dealt with,
The matters of the heart.

How we loved,
Tall and red.
How we fought for,
The ideas, which matter.

We'll remember,
What we saw
How we felt and,
A few words they said
They mattered
Spoke for,
Paved the way
For the rest of our silent lives.

And
We will remember,
The way we smiled.

The way we cared for,
The matters of the heart.
The way we showed up for
The ideas, which sound true.
The way we committed to,
The song of joy.

We'll remember,
A few moments

So long
Yet so short
Shared with other eyes,
Which mattered—
They were found on,
The path of the heart.

Not the rest
Not the rest,
Not those things we did
Because we had to.

But the way we felt
The way we committed to,
The truth of the heart.
Not the rest and
The way,
We made them smile
The laughter
What we shared
And,
The genuine smiles.

Strong soul connections have this perfume, this draw,
this aroma that others simply don't.
They taste like 'I already know you' and we were meant
to do this again. They feel like 'I recognize you'
and here again we were meant to learn.
They taste like soul, like family, like deep knowing
or even blood sometimes.
And no matter where they take us,
how deep goes the unravelling, the storm—
we Know that it was meant to play out exactly
as it did, in the name of higher alchemy,
in the name of mutual growth—
we Know that this was symphony from
the Divine Orchestra.

So long, Love

Dear Lover
Of former times,

This is our last poetry
I believe,
Thank you.

I remember
Our words,
Sacred verses.
Written in green,
Rice fields
My bougainvillea trees in flower.

What a strange impression,
It is
To tell you goodbye,
At last.

Farewell,
Wild dream.

Farewell, goodbye
Dear love
You've been
The One
That smile
Lover of my former times
That smile when I first met you,
You were dressed in white.

The One
You have been,
The mountaintop
The depth of those eyes
Blue
Dear Lover
You have been,

The promise
Of a new life
The spirit
Of hope,

Rhythm of renewal.

That smile,
It was
For a while
The passion of my heart
Then,
An altar candle
A church
A prayer
Dreaming
A last candle,
Waiting
And
Running out of steam
Our last flame,

Goodbye.

✶

So long, love
Life is calling me,
You see.

There are gardens in flower
Riding horses in meadows,
There are walks to invent
Suns, seasons
Life!
Kisses to give back
And,
A soul to offer.

Farewell,
Dear love
May your road be beautiful,

Blue and golden.
And happy-go-lucky
Amused
Light
Ethereal
Joking
Profound, sometimes
Mischievous
Smiling
Playful
Twirling
Blue, of course,

As are you.

And star-spangled
As the Phnom Penh's sky
The mythical set,
Of our love.
Our scenery
Fresco of Apsara dancers
Farewell
That I leave
With you,
It's now time
In this box
Pictures,
Black and white vestige.

In this box of the past twists & turns of my heart
That you turned
Upside down,
For a while
One day
That evening
That beautifully
Irremediably,
In golden sparks.

I let go of,
The invented pictures

The words that were never said
Fly,
Away
You
Disappear, even
Wither.

Dear memory,
My youth vanishes
You were its novel
The blue is turning grey,
Slowly
At last.

I see you flying away
Goodbye,
Goodnight.

Life has its own magic that predictions can't know about

And what is meant to be for the Stars,

Always ends up happening.

Her Skin

Touch her
Like,
She is
The first skin.

Kiss her
Like,
It was always
About
You and Her,
Like
She is everything
Compared to
Every other
Lips.

Hold her waist
Like
She is,
The treasure
The gem
The velvet
You've been
Dreaming of
Waiting for,
Longing.

Kiss her
Like,
You always knew.

Kiss her
Like,
There was never
Anyone else
Like She.

Caress her
Like
She is a diamond,
And
The treasure
Is now found.

Place one hand
On her heart
As if,
You held the keys.

Touch her thighs
As if,
Your hands
Were magic
As if,
You could open her
Her mystery
Her depths,
Because only you always could.

Let your hand
Wander
Over her eyes
As if,
You could read in their glint
That,
You and she are One
And that,

It's Her.

Kiss her heart
As if
She was yours
Because
She's always been since
The dawn of all these magical times
The magnificent hours that were,
Waiting.

Make love to her
As if,
Life had only been
The rehearsal of this dance,
Your dance.

Caress her skin
As if,
You always knew.

Make love to Her
Because
It was written and
Love her,
As deep as life is because
She is the jewellery box of yours
And this,
Was set in stone.

Love her
Because
There is no other depth
That matches
Your strength
In this way,
That well.

Dive in her
As if,
No skin
Could melt with yours
Set that fire in your closed,
Solar eyes.

Make love to her
As if,
There was
No other softness like She.

Love her,
Because
She will highlight you as no other soul could

And,
Inhale her
Because
This intensity
This mystery
This strength
This magic
And this smile of hers,
Is You.

Love her
Because
She would never be,
In your shadow
But only be
The,
Your Queen and
Love her
As if,
She is the treasure
The Sun
Your sunrise
Your dawn,
And you both
The eternal spark

Love.

I believe that through time,
we progressively lose the superficial layers of skin
that were not truly ourselves.

The Dismantling

Underneath it all
Tonight,
There is,
At last
The excitement for Sacred purpose.

We are found.

That voice
So deep, insistent and persevering
It rises from the basement of your soul,
That voice
She couldn't leave you at peace,
Years and months of wondering
She shook you to your core,
Tore you apart
Dismantled your life
Because she knew,

You're of the Sacred Blood.

You now stand
White ground.
Star-studded vacuum,
Gaping hole of light
On this empty frame,
You stand.
Strong and wise,
Seed of stars.

It's the passion for Sacred Love
Dear Heart,
That caused your dismantling.
Such a slow, accurate and violent crime
Of all your past lies,
The slaughter of all the old masks.

You never gave up, Sacred Ritual.

You are now naked
Lighting up the dark night,
You are being knighted
Galloping in a rainbow night,
The road is yours.

Can you hear it?
We are found.

Go back to work,
Burning Hero
Write, sing, build, do, act
Help, speak or open ways.

The dismantling has cleaned you out of the impure, sullied blood.

Now, the gold of the Tigers
Flows in your veins.
The torch of the Phoenix
The Ambrosia of the resurrected,
You rise.

You're lifted up by a new order,
And even your twirling mind
She now acknowledges,
Who you are.

Burn bright, Hero
Old programming has died.

You're brandishing the sword of the Gods,
You're of Service.

✶

Soldier,
You're the Sun in this Moon's sky
The star among the stars
You walk,
Proud and certain of your Heart
General,
Major.

See,
Turn over for an instant:
It's the magic of your eyes that they are following,

You Are An Army.

‘You are not finding your voice.
You are remembering.’

—VICTORIA ERICKSON

Inspirations

'She is an old soul with new style, who wears black and speaks her mind. So powerful—she leaves her prints on everyone she touches because she is both: a savage and a sweetheart.'

—SYLVESTER MCNUTT

Breaking Free

One day, after I have unlearned all the boxes choreographies, I will dance with wings. After I have run from all the normal people's paths. Stopped recounting stories heard outside of my heart, I will write my own script.

One day. When every inch of the former life is gone. When all—what I used to be—is lost. I will sit under the Moon, breathe the Stars and think:

It is time to BE.

It requires much more strength and inner power to do what you are doing, or envisioning, than any of the rest.

It will ask of you a lot more. Not a lot more wealth, titles, labels, and positions. But a lot more courage, faith. Knowledge of the self, perseverance. Commitment, calling.

It will ask you a lot more, but this you have.

It will require a lot more from you, but that is exactly why you are here.

You can resist things. You can, and you could always change your mind but that would only delay your destiny and, destiny always finds us. It plays tricks and music and memories, to find its way back to your heart, you see.

You are brave, this is why you are here.

Life has more in store for you if you follow the path.

You can resist, but it would wake you up at night. The truth, the dreams, the ache of that missing, lost, gone wildness.

You can turn back. You always could.

Interestingly, if we take a look back, you never did.

Interestingly, if you take a closer look at those things of your past—you never lost that smile, those desires. That fire, the melody of the explorer, the longing. That is because of who you are.

It requires much more strength from you to do what you are doing but, that is your path.

The path less travelled, for you, is the Main Road.

Warrior, keep going.

This is your story. This is your life.

Don't look back.

Don't let yourself be pulled here and there, by energies coming from the outside.

Instead, find at your own pace, that place of stillness within. It knows what to do, who to love, which life to live.

As long as we resist the pain, or the truth,
the heart healing and therefore the light,
which so many desires to enter it, are blocked.
And we stay stuck in things that aren't our true self,
our highest good, sometimes only to avoid
a few moments of 'truth'.

Start where you are.
Don't reschedule change.
Move with what's possible.

DON'T THINK of what you should do, who you should pretend to be, to be accepted.

Find yourself first, and then go to the world. When you get there, be who you truly are, and see what comes.

These things, those people—they are your Tribe.

IT IS HARD to be happy with the people we can't be ourselves with.

ON THE PATH, warriors may meet obstacles because they need to 'rise against', in order to rise.

They need to feel a burning *no* in their guts when life or others try to direct them somewhere they don't belong.

Battlefields, my dear friend, give birth to identities.

YOU WON'T be able to silence an emotion until you understand its roots. Or you will think that you did, for hours, for days, even for years, and one day it will knock again on your door and say *Hey*. Emotions are similar to cats. They come and wake you up at night to remind you of what you shouldn't have forgotten, and make sure that they will be fully taken care of.

You would see me as a princess, an heiress, a model or a businesswoman. I would picture myself as a medicine woman, a soldier, an artist and a dancer.

You would see climbing all the ego-stairs up. I would picture myself dancing in a long golden dress of the colour of the crown and with a bright smile—one of the kind that only holy prayers give birth to.

You would see me behind working desks while I was spaces, deserts, and trees.

You would see me as a scientist, but I'm a poet.

You would imagine me as a geometer, an organizer or a banker. But I'm a priestess, a defender of the weak and a kind heart.

✶

A few things have expired in me.

There is no written path. The path is the way we show up out there and express our personality. The path is what we choose to do. It changes if we evolve, it becomes something else the moment we decide to create something different.

The path is not an outside thing set in stone that we have to search for. It is simply what we give our time, and energy to.

The path is, ultimately and surprisingly. What we create, what we decide. What we do.

We listen to others so deeply that we could change our minds, only when we are unsure of what we think.

It requires courage and strength to walk one's own way when the vision is different.

It requires a spirit of bravery to quit and walk towards one's true self because this often times means walking alone, without the support of the communities we were used to, their rules which became once upon a time our public identities, our safety nets.

It requires a mad amount of personal power to walk toward one's true freedom because often times, at least for a while, the warrior has to walk alone a path with no trail—and there, resilience and faith can be found nowhere but in their heart.

Change is allowing new insights to be heard,
as well as the stamina to follow through.

I would refuse all kind of distractions. I had to feel, utterly.
Like a prayer made in the dark night of a church,
the discomfort of being where I didn't want to be
and of bending my desires, my ways, to please others.

I had to remain more to feel the breathless cries of my heart.
The tears, the ache of lying. The madness of knowing that
I could live and give so much more to life probably elsewhere,
but couldn't.

I had to feel my death, almost. Because I knew, I remembered—
that only from such pain and orange inner scenery of flames,
the path of Freedom could be born.

✶

Only from the chaos of unalignment
the canvas of a new world can be born.

Sometimes, I had the feeling that my life had always been about the same thing. Finding the strength to detach from the realities, which didn't feel right to me, even if I had mates, a common ground to sit in and I could relax on a seemingly soft cushion. And even if that actually meant to walk alone, and the roads less travelled.

But each time, same story. They wouldn't change.

It was me, the key—and I had to go.

It is always the one who doesn't like it and who wants to leave, that has to go.

At each important new layer of ourselves, it feels like reaching a new land of mysteries. Unchartered, fresh, never touched or seen. Relentlessly taking us to deeper and to more, with no words. Foggy, it lacks words. A world within is calling, yet it doesn't exist. And so we allow ourselves to go, curious and free.

That is the path of growth. It is, as all things of nature, punctuated by the seasons of being anew. Of rebirth, of whiteness. Of Spring restarting.

We think that life is only those big things that we plan and work toward, those big roadmaps we draw through the years. Those organized plans and strategies that we focus on in order to build.

But actually, sometimes life is the matter of the sparkle of a minute. Of an instant.

We suddenly have a new idea and if we act on it, it may become our next adventure. And we are carried—just like that—to our next chapter.

We cross path with someone after landing somewhere we arrived almost magically, through a strange succession of events and seemingly not important crossroads and decision points—and he becomes our favourite song, the only music a heart can sing.

Trust can only be born under the cover of darkness. Not under the light, where all is seen and recognised.

We are like the Moon, forever evolving but actually, that's how we are characterized, defined.

We are defined by the fact of being forever waning and waxing, forever growing. Forever anew. Tirelessly allowing or releasing something. Forever different but precisely finding consistency, identity, definition, meaning in the journey itself. Trusting only the frameworks of movement and growth, forever changing.

After one's heart cracks open and they begin to Feel, there is no way back. As they now follow the path of feeling their way in life, they become Who they are.

I remember the energy of demolition and loss that I felt on that day when I left what I used to call home, knowing that a chapter was closed and that I'd never come back.

Sometimes we do things and even if we are completely immersed in the action of it, we can feel their power. Their depth. The impact they will have, draw to the future like a thick, undeletable thread.

I knew I was feeling a life behind me, not more but not less. I remember packing fast, disorganized, taking all my things, closing all the cupboards, the doors, the possibilities.

Metaphorically I think I destroyed the furniture, burned the house and so I took the road with everything I kept and all the memories, and drove.

I didn't know where I was going and that is why precisely why it was so strange. Freeing, mad, energetic. Unreasonable, blind, limitless. So I just drove. Liberated and destroyed, solidly anchored in the air, in the nothingness.

Sometimes I would look behind in the wing mirror. Was it to check the impossibility of turning back? I would look back and see that yes, the house had indeed all burned and nothing was left there, and so there was no way back. No way back at all.

I just needed to go now. Drive a little more in that unknow I had built. I had left home without knowing where I was going and I was there driving in a no man's land of unknown people, it was raining all around, and nobody was there to say *hey* on the road, and the car was full of things I didn't even care of and I didn't know where I was going, but forward was the only place to go.

There is no real destination that we can have in mind
in order to sort things out in advance
and build a clear, infallible plan—
but the actual place where we'll land
when we've done all that we had to do.

When we say, 'follow the flow', we think that the dilemma the flow is supposed to solve may be about going to the groceries or not, kissing someone or not, waking up at 8 or 9.

But actually following the flow can be massive too. The flow isn't always pretty and cute and soft, sometimes it is a raging sea and its words speak in letters of fire.

That's how I got divorced soon after getting married, disappeared from places on the other side of the world as if it was a matter of life and death, quit activities and changed career.

Sometimes ruptures and breakthroughs happen fast, and almost all of a sudden what seemed aligned a few weeks before feels one morning like a photo album. A bunch of photographs of important days, and it's like we see them from the bird's eye view. Observing, from the roof almost, we are there yet we are not.

We are like observing Owls in a talking night sky, turning the pages of an album of black & white photographs. Remembering how it felt, who we were on that day, what we thought at that time, what was said and what was true—yet sensing a bit disappointed and lost that we aren't in those sentiments anymore. They are pictures, memories, flashes to revisit but where we are now, the layer we inhabit is different.

There is a distance, a disconnect.

And when this kind of evolution is felt in the heart, we know that changes are imminent.

Even if we may doubt it in the now, life always ends up proving that a gut intuition was right, and that the inner guidance system was reliable.

Paradoxically, it's by freeing ourselves from society's *have to, should be, should wear, think and do*—that we find our true personal power. Our own beauty, essence, magic.

Trying to fit in, be respected or accepted from the outside actually takes us away from the true, mysterious, search... which is finding ourselves. Finding our own ways, our favourite clothes, our essence and our own unique preferred things.

Paradoxically it's by freeing ourselves from obligations and *shoulds*, those things we do because we have to, because it's aligned with trends, because it's commonly seen as *good*, because others expect it, value it or see it as *right* —that we find ourselves. And from there, from the radiance of the within found and revealed... we get to shine and rise, outwardly.

We travel far away, to no man's land sometimes, where all is different and strange and unknown. Where all landmarks are gone and all the easiness of being in the familiar is lost because we need to feel deeply and utterly what exactly we have inside of ourselves.

Because there, there is nothing to hang on to but ourselves and in those faraway spaces of loneliness, of external void, we get to find our strength—life forces us to find who we are.

Trusting is an art. Trust is white magic.
Trust will be your everything.
Trust will be your first smile in the morning,
Trust will be your evening prayer.
Trust will be your favourite song.
Trust will be what you are brought back to,
when you start wondering, forcing things,
doubting your unfolding.
Trust, now, will be your everything.
Because, you know what you're leaving
but, in truth—where you're going is the Unknown.

✶

I've learned that the deeper growth happens
in the dark and in the soul, inwards,
when we are lost and alone and without landmarks.
When life brings us back like a crazy wave
to the core of ourselves.

When I remember all the things I did or quit
in the name of the 'truth',
or shall I say of my authentic self,
I hope that the Truth was informed
and that she has a generous hand.

Sometimes I had the feeling that we were all sharing our own experiences, but ultimately nobody knew what was going on and what the right path was, if any.

Ultimately, I saw that nothing matters but the truth, the healing of my soul. Some days I wanted to be more beautiful, to see my hair blonder or to feel fitter. Some other nights I wanted a shelter to sleep with, or my people next to me. Or I wanted them erased, buried, as much as the thoughts of them would madden in persecution that guarded heart of mine in this very specific now.

But then I saw that none of that was truly the solution to my inner troubles.

Neither my heaven nor my hell, was outside of me.

My life was actually a set of walking holograms, which I'd either adore, sanctify or escape from. I had almost no middle ground and they were only reflecting my own perceptions of an instant reality.

I decided to write to give a meaning to the mess.

I decided to write to keep track of a story.

I decided to write in case it would help understand.

I decided to write to keep track of a process.

I decided to write to make sure that at least on paper,

him & I would live.

Joy

Don't seek something, or someone, but seek Joy—
as a feeling within,
as a vibration inside,
as an energy.

While it is beautiful and good to have ideas, wisdom, and a vision, on the other side of things what truly enables change in the physical, what makes the Vision become Real—is committed action, finding ways to anchor what purpose and truth feel like to a viable ground.

Out of the boxes, there is Freedom,

And the Responsibility to create the right conditions in order to keep it.

At the beginning of everything Freedom is obtained, almost sword stolen, won by the courage of a warrior's heart, it's the matter of an instant—but later it has to be kept, worked for, nurtured, watered, grown, protected.

Change in the physical says long-term devotion to making it happen, and a heart committed to doing what has to be done...to see ideas become stones, and words become reality.

When I began to find my happy, I stopped worrying about what other people think. The way I looked, if I was wearing lipstick or not. If that day I looked elegant, aligned with others, in accordance with the trends. If I was how I should be.

So I started wearing only pants of many colours. I made my hair more golden in case I'd miss the sun. I forgot about diets and being careful.

And, rewards that only joy can bring, I felt more and more comfortable in my body, sexier and the smiles of that new me would always bring sparkles to my eyes, sparkles, and tears sometimes, but always light and deep at the same time.

And that smile was worth a million tricks or trendy plagiarisms to be seen.

Sometimes I'd write for days and sometimes I hated it. I had hours when I wanted to become a novelist or a poet for the mystics and some other times I was mad at myself for such exuberance.

Within me, and as for love, and feelings and all those things that wave and burn and twist, ignited by the flame of passion in my heart, nothing was settled.

Things always had that little funny acid, almost childlike taste of the unpredictable.

Freedom can't be tamed, it is meant for that. It is not meant to grow an outcome.

Freedom just is, just happens, as my writings did.

And so, I couldn't rely on this, as forests don't count on butterflies to build trees and, anyways, my words couldn't settle, sit, they needed to breathe like the wind. To fly, untidy, flowing.

They couldn't learn how to speak the language of the Trees.

It is funny to see that as we change, we see others, stories and the world differently in time while actually nothing truly changed.

It is us, always, and our glasses of the world, which transform.

And that made me wonder a few times if actually any of what happens is real.

Once upon a time, I wanted to write about life, to teach about life or to preach about what it should be. But the day came when I saw that actually, I just wanted to live and be happy.

But my inner world got so rich in time, I couldn't really read or watch movies or things anymore. It felt like I was escaping myself to go elsewhere than in my own temple of stories, words and possible adventures and I didn't want that anymore.

It felt so much better to sit in silence within, listen to the waving melody of my feelings or during summer I'd stare at the Moon and read in its blue and constant reflection (do Moons die? I'm wondering), a few possibilities of what could be.

The greatest freedom, for me,

became the freedom of thoughts.

At the beginning of everything, loving oneself is done through offering ourselves outside things that we think we deserve. Trying to find love, prosperity, excitement, adventure. Somewhere, through other means.

One day, it changes. Loving oneself starts to happen between oneself and their own heart, soul, body.

It's not anymore, *I'm going to give you that thing or take you to that person so you can find joy or relief.* But, *come dear heart, rest in my own arms, tell me how you feel. You and I, we are strong and kind, I'll take care of you as if you were my best, favourite, sacred partner. My most beautiful art, my preferred lover and friend.*

I REMEMBER feeling weird and mad almost my first thirty years of this life. My dreams were too big, my heart was too large. Those were my weaknesses. I was too different, naturally, it was impossible for me to fit in but I would do anything to prove myself that I could.

Everything in my life changed when I understood that I was only the way I was.

So I decided to embrace my personality, to say what I truly thought about things and our world and to never stop or settle before I found the aligned things.

I committed within to keep seeking—until things feel right.

I decided that if I felt that another way existed, then it was accurate.

And so, the weaknesses of my youth became my power. It became the way I became.

The more I would embrace my madness, my strangeness, the way I had to be different, the more I was finding my people and my strength. Not strength like 'show off' or 'look at me', not the power which comes from those things that we only do to be seen or to please the mold of others. No, strength from feeling that I could create and become from what truly resonates within, from knowing that I could be both in the world and true to my intimate, deep, core self.

As WE WALK the path we discover more and more truths about many things. We dig something out, think it is the most powerful ever. And then we change our minds. And we see things differently once more, and again we feel that yes, this may be the thing.

We are funny and so, it's better to keep walking with an open mind and to remember that even the biggest truths can be temporary—as the different spirals of some butterfly's wanderings.

Build yourself yes,
but in a way that respects your Truth.
Or the house will collapse
with the first winter winds.

When we are happy and feel aligned with our lives, we feel more full and so we don't get triggered that much by other people.

From that space of completeness and joy within, we can come from the heart almost with everyone.

How strange. How silly.

If you want to build newness in your life, go for it. Concentrate your energy to create the new, instead of attaching to what doesn't feel right anymore or wondering if you should take pieces of what you're moving away from, with you.

If you want to see newness in your life, move toward it. Don't wait that long. Take the steps, one at a time. Create a new trail. Don't look back that much. You've already decided.

Pause every stone on the way to breathe, regroup and gather your strength perhaps. And if you are still inspired, keep walking. A little more. Slow but steady, certain, confident.

In time, your little adventurous stones become a path and the path, your days and the days—the real story of your life.

We seek power and validation outside

in many different ways,

until we find it within.

Engage in things in order to raise your energy, and not for the perceived outcome they may lead you to—even if they seem like nothing, even if it is just about relaxing or listening to music.

Some days your work for yourself and for your journey is just that—finding ways to come back to your heart, and to that center space in you which knows, senses, aligns and therefore manifests the brightest life for you.

What makes us look beautiful, radiant, and glowing is joy, that genuine sense of what's happening now is truly me—it's aligned, it's my own, self-found, personal, magical, expression of Free.

THE MIND explains but the heart knows.

YOU WALK IN TRUST in your life. Meet obstacles. You struggle and then shine. Someone teaches you, someone makes you smile. Someone holds your hand for a while. Another makes you stumble, and then you come back.

And you keep walking. The way is forward. Always. What else could you do?

And, adventure after adventure, episode after episode, the next chapter is always different from the former. It's a new you, meeting new mirrors, enjoying a new world. Colours are more subtle, new music is found. Places frozen in time, your eyes are different.

And one day, you didn't even plan it, you didn't even see it coming. It seems that you've walked enough because you receive something new, different from all the before. It's beautiful, aligned or big. Life is meeting you too, that's how it seems.

And you smile at yourself—how amazing. That's why I have been walking.

In my twenties, early and late, I was scared of the lonely hours, I was afraid of the night.

The truth is, I didn't know what I really liked doing, so I was scared of being alone, of the void. Of that seeming abyss, endless, frightening question within it would take me to. And as I never wanted to connect with people without feeling a real, sincere, heartfelt resonance or attraction or just to fill in the empty pages of my life, I was scared of the evening. I was afraid of the night.

When I started to find myself, my true soul callings and joy, alone time became absolutely needed, paramount, vital. Those moments were windows to my soul, timid or joyful gates to the mystery inside. Moments not heavily received as they used to, but consciously created, chosen. Those were my writing hours, my healing pages, my nurturing spaces. And others, people—were never seen again as possible escapes out of my complex, sensitive, watery heart.

Nobody knows what sounds like joy, bliss, soul song,

'this is me', gold, I love it, for You—

better than You do,

there, in the deepest of your rainbow soul.

THERE IS NOTHING truly wrong on a healing journey. What seems 'wrong' after a few months or years, from a new and wiser perspective, was exactly what we had to do before and at that time in order to know.

Without it, we wouldn't be where and who we are now. Without it, we would have avoided that learning curve. Without it, all we've figured out and learned since then, we wouldn't know.

And who would we be now, if we didn't learn?

«LIGHTWORK» is more than anything else finding our own path of alignment and bliss, so we do our own part of embodying light and joy in this world.

EVERY LIFE is a Message, even the most private one.

The way we relate to one another, the way we care, the way we love.

The way we commit to ourselves, commit to finding Who we are and Why we are here.

The way we commit to finding our joy, to remembering what makes us feel aligned, alive and free—and the way we commit to keeping it, to growing the good life for a few more seasons and rounds.

The way we repeat to ourselves, over and over again—I Choose You.

The way we align actions and words, the things we decide to do to give birth to what we think.

The changes we make no matter what rules and codes say, the day when the what was becomes unbearable.

The way we physically commit, to what we know at heart is right.

The way we actually listen to the signals of what hurts, of what can't be—the way we commit to walking the adventurous foggy road of Something Else.

The way we decide to spend our time, the things we give energy to. The things we quit and take back our power from, because we Know.

The way we try to align our values and beliefs, what thinks and says the Heart, with the path our feet are actually walking.

The way we fight and commit to, what we think truly matters.

Ultimately the way we commit to creating a life of Joy for ourselves is how we create the message of how a world can be set Free.

WE STRUGGLE as long as we think that we have a spiritual life on one side and on the other a physical existence and needs that would matter less based on a sort of hierarchy. We are here to build Bridges, to create what satisfies all of our parts—what allows ourselves to be Who we truly are but Here.

OFTEN TIMES you absolutely know the way. It's just your mind and its constant thinking and analysis, which confuses you but, always and no matter what happened in between, you come back to it—you Know.

THE MORE YOU walk on the path of finding and embodying the authentic self, the more your body aches when you move in the 'wrong' direction. Listen, those signals don't lie.

Your ideas about what is aligned, and your imaginations of what is truly yours as the 'plan' are clear when the mind is trusting, relaxed, silent servant, on hold.

If we are honest, the most life-changing, magical, next-layer-of-the-soul, transformative unfoldments of our lives were unpredictable by the planning mind a few months before.

The Plan knows other ways.

Sometimes, what will end up being the foundation of a new You comes unannounced.

Self-love is both befriending the inward and finding ways to be happy in the world; a nurturing and all-encompassing presence in our secret and alone empty spaces when awareness expands, emotions are processed and seen and the self needs to be held, as well as giving it the energy and time that it needs to find its sunny place in the great landscape of outward life; the Yin and the Yang; balance; active and restorative—I love you to heal and I love you to become.

A good way to know if this or that idea that I have in mind is truly coming from my heart, and to have the confirmation that I really do it for myself and not for others, is by testing the following *'if I do it but nobody finds it great, if nobody agrees, sees it, knows about it or understands, that doesn't really matter—I did it for me'.*

What is meant to be, always finds a way. That's why it's unnecessary to think of it or to force it.

What is the soul's truth, always comes back. That's why it's unnecessary to let it go.

What is meant to become, always finds its way back to consciousness and to the right action, even if you were busy elsewhere or you thought you forgot.

What's already yours in this life, will be and it asks for nothing more from you but to participate in your own path of alignment and joy.

On that path, it will show up as you go. So you can walk in trust.

Words come and go so fast. They are a soft but restless whisper.
The matter of only one instant, fading like dancer
in a foggy air if not listened to,
if not anchored respectfully on paper.

Almost like a leaf, falling—there is one & only real time
to hear, to receive, to catch them.
It is the sacred instant when an emotion, a memory,
an inner mystery is made words.
Unique instant, fading away as soon as it opened
a secret, unique instant between tree and ground.

The Authentic Self, that core and true part of ourselves is not always what we think, what's presented as the most *enlightened* or new-agey— it is simply what we truly like doing, what brings joy.

You know that someone is a true deep friend when they have stayed in time, even, especially, as you were showing your true colours and unravelling.

That's the core in you they liked, the lotus unfolding.

It is even unnecessary to try and plan the future or see what tonight will be. Because, if we truly accept to stay in presence and gently carried by the river of the now then tomorrow, we may be a different *me*.

The now shapes us constantly, and as a result, the future is.

WE KNOW something is of the authentic self when we enjoy the journey, the process itself, not only a possible outcome.

SOMETIMES I feel that 'awakening' is all about reaching a point where you can fully hold space for fear and let it not guide you, so that you can move freely, tall and happy, in the direction of your truth.

I had a new kind of coffee and thought
I'd never go back to any other.
I went there and thought no place in the world
was that sacred, beautiful.

I found his eyes and then I was doomed.
I couldn't after that, remember the taste of any other lips.

Love

I would have loved that he stayed
but he would always play with us, and with me,
as those most harrowing and red instants of sunsets do,
those instants that only appear in their unique canvas splendour
to show us their take-off.

And it is this ephemeral in him,
this elusive and impossible to catch
which made of his memory such a desired image,
that deeply missed,
waited for.

Sometimes we have to leave the world to find out what we truly think and who we are at heart without being disturbed by any outside voice or interference.

But when we know, when we have found. We are ready to come back.

In the spaces of loneliness I grew, I learned. In the spaces of loneliness, I found my strength. But ultimately I couldn't stay there that long—my most beautiful, striking joys were only lived with others.

People speak about the love that we feel. They tell us who we should love and how we should do it. They tell us that it is ok to love and that it is safe to fall.

But the only force that can solve the immense enigma of love comes from within.

Love must become certain within itself first, or it will shift and twist and turn before it knows, like the waves of a burning sea.

I MISS intimacy so much tonight. Not the kind of togetherness where you speak all the time, debate, argue, complain or share about what other people did.

No, just being with. Staring at the moon, lying down in the grass. Feeling his breathing next to my head, rising with another skin, letting life be. And nothingness flow, and bodies melt and fall in sweet fire, tender like a river. Intense as my heart is, timeless to not wonder where life goes, deep in his eyes and carefree.

You and I breathing in a soaring harmony, forever, again.

IF YOU THINK you are strong and independent just because you have closed your heart to love, you may be wrong. Only by being with another you may discover how tall your heart stands when it starts to burn.

I love you, but I don't want to save you
or to teach you or to solve the equations of your soul.

I love you, but I don't want you to become faster
or that in particular,
and I'm not your journey.

I love you, but I won't try to merge with your thoughts,
to catch you when you fall,
to steal the depths of your descents within,
to introspect for you, to feel for you,
to interfere with the rhythm of your feet.

I love you but I don't want to catch you and I can let you go.

I love you, but I love you as I'd admire a sunny flower
on the other side of the window.

I love you to witness, to walk with you
and as a poet loves their muse
but not to merge
and, there will always be the space of a summer wind
between my heart and your skin.

People like us or they don't, that's the way it is. And even if we'd have liked things to be different, the only real path is of acceptance and seeing things for what they truly are.

And it is sad sometimes when we love whom doesn't love us back but the best way is to see it, smile in our hearts in honour of what could have been, and carry on.

The best way to become our greatest version with Others—the most loving and compassionate; respectful of their own path even if it is a different one; present for them and to share joy but not in need; authentic, spontaneous and detached from the ego needs to prove ourselves right or to be more—is to become our own happiest and most complete version Within.

But you wouldn't be disappointed by others that much if you didn't always expect them to please and fulfil you.

People cross path naturally,
they evolve in togetherness naturally
or they'd rather not.

When we force love, commitment, encounters,
we actually bend life to our will
and think that it is possible to shape destiny on our own.

But destiny isn't that.
Destiny just unfolds, as the Sun everyday rises.

Learn to love, but learn to let go of love when love has passed. Know that, if a person wants to love you, to hold you, to make you smile—they will say it, or do it, so don't let silences make you think that white speaks and, remember that if love aligns, love will flow.

If they made you laugh, smile or touch more joy, then thank the Gods, the Priestesses and the Stars but don't let the memory of beauty make you expect its return, don't let the past stop the pursuit of the soft calling of your today's heart.

If you have a kind heart, a soft soul or an open mind, keep it—but don't let your innocence, that genuine side of yours trap you in the illusion that others are you—and that what is not done, said or explained can always be excused, erased or understood.

Be soft, yes, and be kind, but don't let your own kindness trap you in the golden cages of those who fell in the name of too big of a heart, those who stumbled with the hope of catching a love medal.

Believe in dreams, in magic and signs but don't let the fairy or the angel in you, turn yourself into a novel's heroine, Sleeping Beauty or the prince of a kingdom alive only in the thoughts of your daydreams.

Love, yes. And please, love more, and please, love again.

But learn to see when love has passed, too, and most importantly remember. When a heart wants to love you, to hold you or make you smile—would they be a hero, a painter or a king, a soul of the land or a poet, a shepherd or a violoncellist—they will say it or do it.

They will be there actually, in the daily novel of your life. They will be there, flesh, colours and sound—they will love you, hold you and make you smile.

If only we could love people for what they are,
and not for what they bring us.
If we could love them for where they are at, their ways,
even if they don't match our expectations always and exactly.

If we could love just in the name of love,
and not be filled by someone else exactly as we had planned to.

If we could love people for what they actually give,
and not for what we thought they would say or do or be.
Well, I think in that case,
my heart would always be with You.

✶

The only way to forgive others
is to love ourselves so much that we become full,
and so our love becomes unconditional.

We can only receive love from the outside to the depth that we give it to ourselves.

And we can only see ourselves in the eyes of another to the extent that we've accepted to see and feel the profoundness of who we are.

A relationship becomes truly possible when we've outgrown the heavy and stormy push & pull, the stay or leave, that it makes us feel. When we become capable, in spite of the triggers, to offer consistency.

Sometimes, I have felt that the Universe takes back from our lives the ones that we Love the most, the ones we feel the most connected to, like deeply because—if they were still here, we would just melt in love and forget about the rest. We would just forget about growing ourselves, independently, we would put this on pause. We would just melt into their skin and heart, and become a sort of bubble of light, timeless, expansive and yellow, and stopped in time. We would stop building, creating ourselves. We would freeze our becoming. We would just merge in love, in recognition, in togetherness. We would become 'us'. We would be Too Much. We would stop the path to Wholeness.

See, sometimes it is the Ones we love the most who must leave because, those are the ones we would have been tempted to merge, to melt, to become one with—while One, must be Within.

The most important soul contracts of our paths
come into our lives to help us release the emotional baggage,
the heaviness we came here carrying.
They offer the space for us to let go
of the unhealthy layers and ways we had within ourselves—
they offer the opportunity to let go of the karma,
we came into this lifetime to be liberated from.

Conscious Sex is when a Man enters a Woman with his soul.

He is not there to be the king of the castle or the #1 acrobat of the year.

He is there to give Her his energy and what He knows.

He is there to love her and honour her, as sacred task of Man.

Both are here to land sacredness on Earth, to ground love as the Heart into primal.

Both came here to embody Divine Force in its strength, in its infinite magic, in its wild, unlimited and ecstatic power and force and ground it into what's Real.

He is there to give her the space where she reveals Herself, where she becomes God, life force, where she unites the Four Elements.

He is there to see and receive Her so much, that she just opens and melts into surrendering to Him.

He is there to surrender His warrior's carapace in Her, he is there to become the softness of his given heart and welcome, through her, more of His own soul.

Both have come together to see how the Masculine and the Feminine become One.

He is there to show her, that at least here and now, she could let go and become She.

He is the explorer—longing to touch, to heal and to learn the deepest, most ancient and primal truth of his Empress, from the magical infinity of her temple space.

If you can, if you are able to.
Don't fall in love with a person's potential
who they could be, who they could have been—
who they could have risen, soared into.

If you can, and even if you see the purity of a Soul—
fall in love with a person.
Fall in love with a Man or a Woman.
Words, flesh, actions.
Actual beingness, actual behaviour.

The Princess waits, dreams of being saved, rescued or chosen.
She somehow seeks something from a specific man,
supposed to be her Prince. Sometimes she accuses or blames,
because she was searching something that she needed,
elsewhere—so this external had to be perfect and all right.

Conversely, a Queen is on her own.
She stands, wise and still, so much in herself than her heart
is open, loving and free. She stands and she loves,
as an anthem, a joy or a crown—independently from 'them'
or from 'him', independently from any outside kingdom,
because This is Her. She is both Love and Power,
as an essence or an inner symphony
and, independently from any specific external dances.

So she doesn't blame because she knows that the Creation,
the Womb of her life—is in her.
And she loves, just because of love and not because of need—
just because love is one of her fragrances.

Love is pure, love is flow. Love doesn't cage.
Love is beauty found within wanting to be expressed,
love is an energy of joy and light desiring to be shared.
Love plays and intertwines, but love doesn't attach.
Love does not stop you on your way.
Love does not demand, love does not ask you to choose.
Love supports your growth, your evolution, your path.
Love loves people enough to let them go.
Love does not own.

Love is you expanded and full,
desiring to give, smile, share, heal, receive or play.
Love is to not need to be with, in order to love.
Love doesn't want to make his, to know, to plan or to trap.
Love just is, it is You.
And it expands as you expand, and it touches others—
see, it is your own heart flowing—
as you walk the golden path.

Some stay even when you are in your power, when you show your true colours, when you remember your truth. Some remain even when you stand up for yourself, when you express your desires and needs, when you stay on the line of fully reclaiming your gems, your gifts.

Some stay on board even when you shine, when you sparkle. Some remain even when you get fierce, when you stand up for yourself, for you know is right and good for you.

Some stay even when you drop the shield, surrender the armouring, when you show yourself, flow your heart, speak what shaped you even in the dark. Some stay even when you fall, when you do the wrong thing, when you come from the shadow.

Some stay when you are both in your power and loving—both true to Yourself and your core but soft, open, ready to dance deeper.

Some stay even when you are fully, entirely You—all the pieces.

Those are rare. Those, are the right ones.

As we progressively travel toward more completeness
and inner peace, within,
we learn to love others in the highest ways.

And it is a promise from the ancient times,
that those spiritual warrior ones will find their mirror
and match in another when the Sky says—
it is Time.

And it is a promise from the original sacredness that One
that has explored those same struggles and mystical prayers
of finding the self, of rising in what is Truth,
of deconstructing the lines and barriers of the mould
to create a self-made journey of dirty hands and faith,
of battlefields and freedom, a road of darkness to Kingdoms,

One who also bears the name of Alchemy—
will be there and ready and found,
according to what was already written,
When the sky says—
it is Time.

A few tales from a journey of Self-Discovery

‘A priestess is a woman who helps others connect with the Divine so they can heal or actualize their soul’s unique path.’

—DARA MC KINLEY

'Just like moons and suns,
With certainty of tides,
Just like hopes springing high,
Still I will rise.'

—MAYA ANGELOU

I hope, I create, I become

I hope, I create, I become.

I hope.

I hope I'll get back home before dark. I hope I'll have enough money, I hope I'll get the dreamed job. I hope I'll get there on time. I hope they still have my favourite tea.

I hope I'll find a turquoise blue necklace. I hope I'm his kind.

I hope I'll find joy. I hope I'll become who I am.

I hope I'll get one of the special looks that make you think you've been noticed within a whole crowd. I hope he'll smile at my witticisms.

I hope the system will give me its consent.

I hope I'll travel the world. I hope my parents never die.

✶

I wait.

I wait for the tube, I wait for the evening, for the *Thank God It's Friday*. I wait for the holidays.

I wait for another day. I wait for summer. I wait for the right day to go running. I wait for a strawberry and champagne evening. I wait for them to see me.

I wait for life to give me the time I need to be me.

I wait for opportunities, for a sign from the Universe. I wait for some kind of positive conspiracy carrying me to my mountains.

I wait for someone to draw me a road, I wait for the stars to line up.

I wait for someone to show me my way. I wait for the right moment to speak the truth.

I wait here before I shine. I wait here before crazy encounters.

I wait here before life starts.

✶

I'm still waiting.

And here she comes. She is a glowing gypsy. She looks feathery, free and airy—her hair is singing in the wind. She is all golden, sparkles in her eyes, freckles on her cheeks, coloured jewels tinkling softly. As if stars had decided to meddle in each of the empty parts of her body.

She says,

Follow your intuition, listen to your powerful word, even if it drives you to unpredictable paths. Don't be afraid of challenges. Give it a try, learn; sometimes you'll fall, but you'll get back on your feet.

You're here to learn—learn until you know enough, learn until you become yourself. Don't remain on the mainstream road if it's not yours.

✶

She leaves but shows up from time to time in different forms, such as a bird's nest under the house roof, clovers pushing through gravels. Dazzling red flowers majestically standing out in the distance of a green valley, old bridge over a mountain stream.

She comes through unexpected smiles, connected people and endless night talks, like hands of destiny.

She says,

Stop dreaming; do. Stop waiting; there'll never be a better time for you. Your time is never, as well as always and now.

✶

Then I start creating.

I create a photo frame. I create a turquoise blue necklace. I create Christmas tree bulbs, I create a poem.

I create my own objectives. I create a new career. I create passion at work. I create my self-taught stuff.

I create love. I create treasured memories. I create bridges towards them, I create my paths to the ones of my soul.

I create my oxygen. I create my time. I create my space. I create my coffee breaks.

I create my faraway escapes. I create my breathtaking sights.

I create my opportunities. I create my inspiring days. I create my art evenings. I create my selfish moments. I create my clouded mornings.

I create my weak afternoons. I create my unreasonable nights.

I create what had always run through my veins. I create what I have been hiding for too long. I give birth to what matters.

I create each day a new step. I create my own project. I create my answers. I create my own rules. I create my weapons against fears.

And whenever she comes back, she says,
Try, keep learning, and become.
And so, I become.

I hope,
I wait
I create,
I become.

'In life, a person can take one of two attitudes: to build or to plant. The builders might take years over their tasks, but one day, they finish what they're doing. Then they find that they're hemmed in by their own walls. Life loses its meaning when the building stops.

Then there are those who plant. They endure storms and all the vicissitudes of the seasons, and they rarely rest. But unlike a building, a garden never stops growing. And while it requires the gardener's constant attention, it also allows life for the gardener to be a great adventure. Gardeners always recognize each other, because they know that in the history of each plant lies the growth of the whole World.'

— PAULO COELHO

The romance of the Gardeners

And she decided she would be a Gardener.

She would be as colourful, as wild, as season changing, as always renewed, as bucolically messed, as full of evolving recesses to explore, as a garden.

Who are gardeners?

Gardeners know that in life, things bloom while another die. They accept it—both in gardens, hearts, and souls.

Every season, every year or every period of time, depending on their own sun and rain rhythm, gardeners have new flowers to grow. New guests come. New ideas bloom.

Gardeners love the rhythm of natural mysteries and their uncertainty. They love going to sleep wondering what colour flowers will display at dawn and how tall new trees will be in a few years' time.

Evidently, they sometimes stop being renewed. Sometimes even forever. When they end up finding their gardens striking, fully aligned as it is—they stop growing new trees.

On some days, gardeners look younger than they are because ideas are still blooming in their minds. Because they don't refuse fresh starts and rollercoasters.

On some days, they seem older and wiser. Because they've seen more, tried more. They have stumbled and failed more. They have been through hotter summers and recovered from more windy, snowy, hermit winters.

But gardeners don't stay away from investment. They build too, but differently. Their now may not be their accurate future and eternal projection, but their choices often require a great dose of courage, efforts, focus, hard work and investment.

They do finish things. They do stay. They do commit if the connection between what they do and who they are at heart is still alive. In that case, they get involved with no boundaries.

If the connection has truly faded, they move. Mostly slowly, gently and carefully with both heart and thought, step by step.

To have a new garden flower again, gardeners know it takes time. It takes a lot of attention, a great amount of Sun, a good dose of water, and possibly a little help from the Stars.

Then, who are Gardeners? Mainly people following their intuition and heart and ready to nourish their soul in spite of its evolution. Ready to fight and work hard to do so, but also brave enough to move on if needed. Ready to let go what is not them anymore and willing to learn. Ready to change.

She thought, *I'm one of Them.*

We can fight anything in this life,

sometimes even for years,

but the truth of the soul.

A TALE OF A SPIRITUAL JOURNEY

This path of enlightenment is like being on a Train. It always changes. The sceneries and colours around you, what people say and do.

Sometimes the train moves slowly, softly, like a river. It is giving you time. You regroup, smell the flowers and contemplate.

And all of a sudden, it stops somewhere new. You are at a New Station. You were ready for it.

There, the weather is different. Something requires more of you. There is a feeling of more aliveness available, more joy—but it seems that it will also require a shattering. Or an initiation, perhaps a rite of passage.

✶

And you get to choose—whether you stop there to explore and taste that country, or if you ask for a little more time before jumping. If it feels too soon, you will get onto the next. The beauty is, growth—trains are not a one-time thing.

There, in that New Country, people speak a language that is even closer to your soul. You are a little surprised, but beautifully. They have new dreams compared to what you heard of before—dreams that are yours.

✶

They speak to a deeper layer of truth in your eyes. They see the world in the same letters of light.

But the train keeps going, always. And you can see that much is changing, often, around you. Not only the sceneries. The people too. Some simply come and go in your life.

Because at each station, new people get in. Those share that same eagerness of yours, a same moment on a journey, that same calling. Some others leave at each stop, they don't come back up in the train with you. For them, that place was a destination.

And you, as you keep going, you can see that you are travelling through a succession of Edges.

Your mind is so often reshaped, your body releases burdens as you travel breakthroughs. Those edges you move through are found within the self, but once embraced they take you to new tangible stations. There, you meet new worlds, embrace new people or new things. Those seem to be outside of yourself—they actually represent a layer of You.

It is the nature of the edges itself, that keeps you going. The taste of it. The fragrance of expansion, of Growth.

So you keep going. You had signed up for it, it seems. Your desire and your curiosity are still alive, fresh, young—even after all those former adventures and the multicoloured ups and downs.

The thirst is still alive. Something in you still yearns for more. Like at the very beginning. You have visited many countries already but, the song of more within you has remained the same. Unaltered, hungry—electric, certain of itself.

✶

Something in you, is never tired of evolving. Something deep down knows that the next stations are right, before the next.

Something in you Knows. And it is ready, one more time—to jump on the train, surrender and close eyes, be shaken and travel to the Next Ground.

Choose joy, be free.
Choose joy, be free.
Choose what makes you feel alive,
what makes you feel good and free.
And repeat.
Be unleashed, untamed and revealed.
It doesn't have to be conventional,
it doesn't have to be what you did.
Get wild, get real, be you.
Untamed, uncensor yourself.
Become unlocked,
choose what makes you feel good and alive,
and be free.

I Am What I Choose to Become

I decide what I give meaning and power.

In truth, your life is meant to make you feel so inspired and alive with rainbows and sun.

In truth, you are not here to please anyone else but yourself.

In truth, going by the book only matters if the book is yours.

The truth is, you are not here to prove yourself to others but instead, to approve of yourself.

A few affirmations:

I have the power to find my own system of values and to give it as much importance as I give to outside thoughts and beliefs.

I decide what I give power to, and who or what leads my life. Who holds the reigns?

I decide that my purpose is joy with a big J, and only I know for sure what brings me joy.

✶

The beliefs we've received from others (education, ancestors, friends, society) have as much power on ourselves as we allow it.

They are not ours even if it feels that they are and our work is PRECISELY to work on seeing and releasing what IS NOT individually aligned and in resonance.

'The soul is always individual; mind is always group, any mind, watch carefully, and you will find it belongs to some group.'

—OSHO

Becoming who we truly are mean discerning what's ours and what isn't, and letting go of the undesired baggage—those things that we think are our personal wording about life, but which actually don't come from us.

✶

If there is one thing that we as humans are in the capacity of defining for ourselves, it's the way we think.

If there is one thing that we as humans have the power to give birth to in our own most intimate and personal way, it's the way we see life.

If I walk in life from my most personal core of what's right, I leave a trail—most likely new—by writing my story as I feel personally inspired and called to.

If we decide to take others' point of view for universal truth, we align with it and actually start to play by rules that are not ours. What is personal fulfilment?

There is immense power in finding our own rules because from there, no matter what we do, it is right.

We don't punish the soul or force the heart—instead, we bond so tightly with loving the self.

We don't beat ourselves up to 'make it work' in case being soul-happy would make us fall—instead, we allow the core to emerge, grow and lead.

We just follow the inner guidance, what makes us feel the most in joy, inspired, responsible of every word of the journey, in mastery, on a mission, driven by the core, by the guts.

Alive.

The creator.

I give shape to the path,

Driven by an intimate, personal anthem of what's meaningful.

I Travelled Only to Come Back Home

For a very long time in my life I thought—joy is somewhere. Joy is in Paris. No, joy is in Cambodia. After all, no, joy is in the green, in the country.

Joy was somewhere. In the mountains or maybe by the sea or maybe in a specific country. There was a place and, some day I'd be able to put my finger on it.

So I travelled, I travelled a lot. It was neither truly the East nor the West, the answer wouldn't be that straightforward.

Everything was beautiful, nothing was perfect. The answer was everywhere and nowhere at the same time.

✶

Eventually, I saw that Joy was something that we tap into, within.

Eventually I saw that the spell of joy is inside and so, joy was always available.

All the heavens and the hells, they were inside of me.

I was luck and despair on my own—freedom, brightness or stuckness on my own too, and I could be any of it anywhere.

✶

No, joy was neither Paris nor it wasn't. Joy didn't have to be found in Cambodia, but joy was there too. Joy was near the ocean sometimes, joy was seeing a sunset, joy was also the foreign, the wild or skyscrapers some other days.

Strangely, even if I was evolving and was almost something different after all the rest—joy was always available in my pink hometown, my French Toulouse city.

✶

Eventually, joy was like a door in my belly that I could find and tap into, from anywhere.

Joy was found Within. Joy was unshakable somehow, because I started to know its path, its road inside.

Joy was everywhere because it was an inner thing.

All the Heavens and the Hells, all the colours of an energy spectrum—it was me.

I like to be awake during the night
because nobody expects you to do anything.

Only the Moon watches.

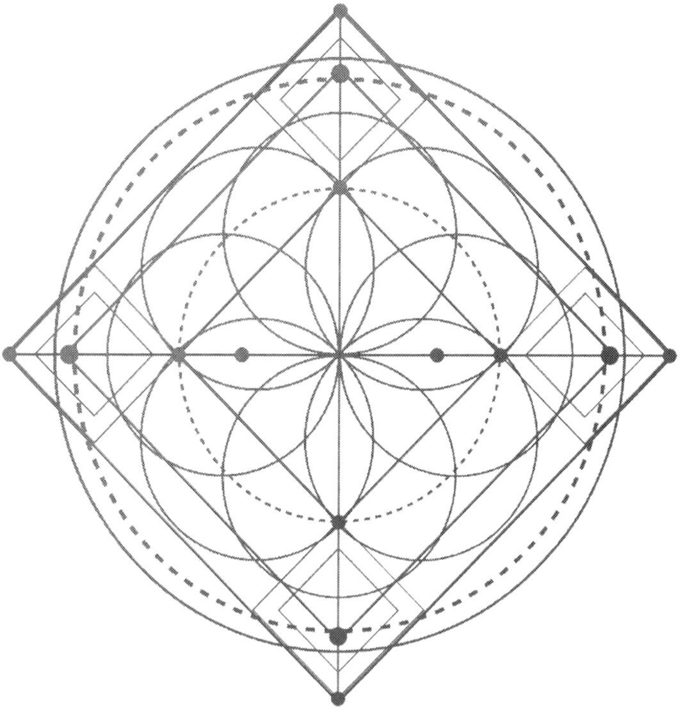

About the Author

SOPHIE is a spiritual seeker and intuitive healer. She believes that our main purpose in life is joy—and that our joy is found in being, or remembering, our authentic self. Her passion is to help spiritual seekers connect to their purpose and reclaim their inner ability to live their own greatest life. Sophie has discovered her intuitive gifts and wisdom through a continued journey of love, of worldwide explorations and of constant introspection and self-realization in order to heal. Her work focuses on empowering others through a broad healing approach which reconciliates the contributions of spirituality and of science-based knowledge.

Printed in Poland
by Amazon Fulfillment
Poland Sp. z o.o., Wrocław

62104352R00096